NORMANDALE COMMUNITY COLLEGE
9700 FRANCE AVENUE SOUTH
BLOOMINGTON, MN 55431-4399

FIVES

PHILIP DACEY

SPOON RIVER POETRY PRESS

1984

This book is printed in part with funds provided by the Illinois Arts Council, a state organization, and by the National Endowment for the Arts. Our many thanks.

Copyright (C) 1984 by Philip Dacey. All rights reserved. No portion of this book may be reproduced in any form without written permission of the author, except for quotations embodied in articles and reviews.

Published by Spoon River Poetry Press, P. O. Box 1443, Peoria, Illinois 61655. Typesetting and printing by M&D Printers, Henry, Illinois.
first edition

ISBN 0-933180-63-2

ACKNOWLEDGEMENTS

Thanks to the editors and publishers who made possible these poems' earlier appearances in print as follows:

Back Door: Mail; The Lovers

Chouteau Review: Marginal Existence

Coming Together: Love Poems (Pflaum): The Lovers

Epos: Kitchen Poem

FallOut: The Position

Four Nudes (Morgan Press): The Nude

The Greenfield Review: Not Correcting His Name Misspelled on the Mailing Label

Kansas Quarterly: Men-strual

The Lake Street Review: Arriving Late for a Movie

Loonfeather: The Pianist

Lower Stumpf Lake Review: Detroit

The Midwest Quarterly: The Descent

Nebraska Review: The Female Impersonators of Bourbon Street

New Jersey Poetry Journal: The Earache

The New York Times: Staying Thin

Outerbridge: One Year

Poet Lore: Breathless

Poetry Northwest: Five Senses: A Bestiary

Seneca Review: The Body

Southern Poetry Review: The Racing Form

Sou'wester: Hands

Spectrum: The Richmond Tri-Annual Review: The Nude

The Spoon River Quarterly: Lament for a Dentist

Sundog (Minnesota): Mobius

Telephone: The Laughter of the Gods

Tar River Poetry: Lines

for Fay

who made us five

In biology the number 5 crops up more than its share of times. Practically all land vertebrates have five fingers and five toes on each limb. Even the horse has five: Its hoof is really an enlarged fingernail of a specialized middle digit. Many marine animals, including sea urchins, sand dollars, and sea cucumbers, have fivefold symmetry. Most modern starfish have five arms. There are fossil remains of starfish that aren't five-armed, but they have all died out.

Most flowers have five petals, and even those that have many more, such as the daisy, have an underlying fivefold symmetry. Many fruits show the quintessence of their ancestry: Cut an apple, a pear, or a banana crosswise and you'll see the seeds are arranged in a five-pointed star.

> Scot Morris, *Omni* magazine

Five is
the human soul. As that soul
holds within itself all the world's
contrarieties, male and female,
good and evil, night and day,
so is five the first number
holding odd and even.

> Schiller, *Piccolomini*

I

NOT CORRECTING HIS NAME MISSPELLED
ON THE MAILING LABEL

Daley. I'm that one, too,
or ought to be. Daily.
Diurnal. To die earnestly
into the hour, the urn shaped
like a woman's body

that turns over and over,
lover to lover,
tireless hole
into which the universe
rushes, dallying. Dali

at work, melting time.
Quotidian, too,
no tedium, quite,
all queynt
and caper. Once,

for months, I was Decay.
The mail got to me, the vowels
dancing their round.
I've never been Decay since.
Now I want to be Cyaed,

a Welsh verse form
impossible to pronounce,
a near-forgotten
arrangement of sounds
some few mouths can enjoy.

STAYING THIN

What it comes down to
is this:
a line.
You are that line.
You can

sign yourself on it,
giving away your life,
or you can walk it,
performing an act
high above the crowd.

It is a matter of passage:
to go through the eye
of a needle,
to slip into the
toughest locks.

And there is always
the old-time movie
you are trapped in:
at the height of the chase
you turn sideways

and thousands of policemen,
of friends, of lovers,
race past you,
thinking you are only the sign
of a man.

THE PIANIST

The keys were rolling
under his fingers
and he followed them,
followed with his whole body
the fingers following the keys.

And the keys... they followed the music
that was hiding a touch away
and hoping to be found
before the sun went down
and all were called in to supper, or bed.

One thing led to another
not-thing. The music couldn't be seen,
even when found. He had to believe in it
like any ghost
to give himself a past,

that is, a future.
He was in between,
surrounded even,
the black piano like a night
and he the day

travelling, listening
to himself get something
out of nothing, the great
resonating chamber
like a heart, and hammered home.

THE DESCENT

What I wait for
is a horse parachuting
from the skies,
his hooves pawing
the air,

his belly caught
up under a sling.
It would take years
for the descent.
Each day of my life

I would look up
to see the wild,
dark eyes
grown slightly
larger,

moist with sadness
and confusion.
As he floated
nearer, I would
notice the almost

human face:
by now centuries
out of heaven,
this oddity,
this brother.

THE FIVE SENSES: A BESTIARY

the small dog of the nose
rummaging in the wind
a stray
he never gets
anything substantial

mouth
belly of a little
leviathan with a taste
for Jonah
who can no longer be found

the ears a pair of birds
they want to lift
the head off
and fly it back
to heaven

the curled brown bears
of the eyes
when they dislike what they see
they say it is winter
and sleep in a cave

fingers a tangle
of snakes one rears up
from the ground
and points at you saying
we would nest in your hair

II

BREATHLESS

He got caught in a wind once
and went with it. No one saw him
for as long as the wind lasted.
Then he came back looking
like someone who'd been somewhere.

Those who stayed asked him where,
but there wasn't a wind
in their words, and he said, Huh?
There was something blowing
in his ears their words couldn't master.

For years afterward he held his
thumb out and stood by the side
of every conversation. The crotch
collected things — a rosary, a hat,
a nest a bird left like an investment —

but what good was all that
to take him to the next town
on the map he imagined, the one that
once unfolded could never return
to itself, the map that budded open?

Finally, he studied sails, theory
and practice, until he grew expert
enough to hoist above all his prayers
the most elaborate sort. Breathless,
he stumbled under their weight.

MARGINAL EXISTENCE

Here in this white space
we can have a party.
What book is this?
Without us,
the text would bleed

into oblivion.
Do you hear a spine
cracking?
Right now,
someone is making

marginal comments
on us.
Does it tickle?
Does it wound?
We're cornered

and numbered
but we go up
and down
and all around.
If this is poverty,

no one can say
where we end
and what's written
between the lines
begins.

ARRIVING LATE FOR A MOVIE

If you miss the beginning,
you miss the end.
The end
is in the beginning.
There are signs

at the very start
as to what the final
scene will mean.
The deathbed that rides
off into the sunset

could be comic or not,
depending on the light
modelling the baby's
emerging head
as the credits begin.

And the fire
in the middle, the beginning
lost, becomes
mere calories,
something to read by,

though the flames
lick the root of the tongue.
Coming in late, you tread
on toes and spill
a handful, a mouthful.

DETROIT

Shut the car door.
Let me hear it
and I'll tell you if
I want to buy it.
The manufacturers

build in a solid
sound to hide
the tin. Thunk.
And all America
shudders with delight.

Nothing can get in
or out, all borders
sealed, the car
as condom,
for this trip

we're safe-
encapsulated,
Heart, no leaks
to lessen us,
me at the wheel,

you hugging the glass
to see the dying
world, contagion
on its lips, a lover's,
beautifully pass.

LAMENT FOR A DENTIST

The teeth
are falling
everywhere
out of heads.
The mouth of God

will soon
be empty. Etzkorn
is dead. Etzkorn
is decaying.
Who can fill him

up with himself?
Who can fix
the bite of God?
The face of the world
sags to its gums.

Death has struck
a nerve.
Doctor Death
has come to town,
the new dentist,

he has taken over the practice
of Etzkorn. Weep
for Etzkorn. Weep for us.
Clumsy hands
fish in our mouths.

III

THE LOVERS

It is exactly right
the way we hold hands.
Animals could not
do it better.
The grip

is not unlike wrestlers'
or a couple's
at a ledge, one
hanging over. No,
we don't sit so

melodramatically, but we aren't
settled either.
Our hands are
an African plain
small beasts

run over.
There's always
something doing.
As harmless as a helicopter-
safari, perhaps,

or something darker
rushing from the horizon.
See how each hand
keeps up with the other,
exchanging looks!

THE NUDE

She is my island.
The breasts are full of stories.
Her feet grow
as big as pans.
She is my kitchen

where beans cook.
I can take her apart
and lose pieces of her.
When I sleep next to her
I am amazed

how she is all one.
Birds settle on her
and peck at my eyes.
I am running into her
like a snow-drift.

But she remains
white and the same thing
through all my changes.
Each finger
is as thick as a pipe

I smoke. A cat
sits on her chest.
Who could be better
to swill than this enormous
cool drink?

THE RACING FORM

"I have been partial to women jockeys ever since the time Robyn C. Smith brought a filly named Bel Sheba around seven furlongs at Saratoga, her hair let loose from under her cap and streaming and I thought if I touched it I would burn my hand."

Gary Gildner

And the cap flies off
and then the blouse,
silk rainbow
the wind balloons,
then breeches, boots,

and she's left with
only underthings,
still riding hard,
the whip falls again
and again to the flank

of her naked horse,
and now the pink
top flutters away
and the bottoms tear
easily and ride the air.

O, it is too late
to bet on her!
I watch, through tears,
her body move
with her mount's and cheer

against myself, the wad
I put down on the field.
As she wins, her whip
turns into a snake
wearing the colors of God.

MÖBIUS

Our love
with no inside or outside
or no clear
line dividing so,
a twist

in ancient history
carried crooked
in the blood,
the waves
of our lives

flooding the years.
Now one,
now the other,
where are we,
where were we,

these questions, too,
seamlessly one.
We make a figure
like a circle
but not,

a mouth
under pressure,
a beauty
marred by the motion
of feeding itself.

LINES

The female shape
of a poem.
How to reveal
that curve,
those

curves.
The poem walks
in front
of you,
in-

vites
in tight
jeans. You
married one
once, happily,

but always
the lines return,
new figures rotate
against each other,
grinding to meaning,

and the blood
becomes a word
weighed, in hand,
to woman,
pound for pound.

IV

MEN-STRUAL

"Havelock Ellis suggested that males possess some traces of a rudimentary menstrual cycle."

                          from a book on Victorian sexuality

What was I to make
of the spot of blood
on my jock strap?
Tennis
is no contact sport

and I had just had
my yearly checkup. I was
100%.
But there it was,
a red period at the end

of a sentence I couldn't read.
Twenty-eight days later,
the same period, the sentence
becoming clearer. I loved
the woman I lived with,

but now I began to dream
of rags, of the poverty
of simple thoughts,
and of rich
Tiresias,

condemned to the beauty
of a moon with no side
in shadow, somewhere
a secret sun,
or a light within.

THE BODY

The body always
rights itself.
It will throw
itself on the ground
to right itself.

There is the gyroscope
of the spirit
keeping the body
humming.
Even in death

the body flourishes,
a fireworks beautifully
showering the earth.
It always knows, each pore
an eye,

sighting the right shore
for this particular
trip on this particular
day. It goes there,
the limbs flailing

like a mad
windmill
but actually
the body's
flying.

THE FEMALE IMPERSONATORS OF BOURBON STREET

Which, what, is it,
he, she? The sub-
atomic world
of sex, in-
determinacy.

Atoms have more space than mass,
but try to walk through walls
or girls like these. Small, whirling
particles of dream
faster than the eye can see

keep you out, or in.
Mirror, Mirror,
what's my sin?
When space curves
I want to lie down

in it, part of a circle,
piece
of circumference
the center
takes, love

a quantum quest.
And time runs
at no one speed. I pace
this runway, Boy,
all relative to need.

KITCHEN POEM

The fork is a terrible instrument.
You can tune
a murder on it.
It crosses
knives, the well-intentioned

bleeders
of hearts and thighs.
You pick up
with the spoon
all loose things

and get carried away.
A plate next,
a cameo
of your hungry face.
Your head is on it.

And a cup and saucer.
They rattle.
They are playful.
They come alive
when you throw them.

All these lie exposed
but are not raw
like a wound.
The table edge calmly
circumscribes their ways.

MAIL

The best-class mail
is secret, arriving
at all hours
to change your life,
though you know nothing of it.

And there is the mail
written in code
in your own hand.
You spend years
trying to remember the key.

Some mail gets carried
miles on the back of an animal.
He comes to your doorstep.
He reads it to you.
You go down on all fours.

All mail, whether it says so
or not, is postage-due,
and some of it
returns to you marked
"Sender unknown."

When mail stops arriving,
you begin folding yourself up.
You look for some place
to insert yourself
that will take you away.

v

ONE YEAR

They leafletted our town.
They told us everything
we had to know.
The leaflets were all colors,
a rainbow-snow.

They told us all we ever
had to know
but told in such a way —
how should I say? —
there wasn't any certainty.

The leaflets fell in May;
that fall, their edges
torn and frayed (we'd read
and re-read every one
and carried them around

the way some men
carry cards that bear
their names), we mulched
the garden with them.
In spring, the damned-

est things came up.
And yet we took
a pleasure in each one
(who knows why?) and cock
an eye now toward the sky.

THE EARACHE

It was somebody
trying to say something
or something
without a name
hoping to tear one

from me:
the ear filled
with an unknown substance,
a lode, mother
or father

or neuter wish,
a bud
of pain
I waited to hear
bloom,

till even ow
became a way to say
hello, be my guest,
to the alien
love

come to play
the difficult music,
the future,
bell, belle,
to strike to tell.

THE LAUGHTER OF THE GODS

The laughter of the gods
echoes through hills,
down the clouds,
lodges in trees,
imitates birds.

The wind is a leftover
laugh, the tail-end,
the only part of a comet
we can see, the sign
there was a joke here.

What else do they have to do
all day, the gods, as important
as that roll, that tumble
of comedy into turbulence?
"Storm," they say. "The biggest laugh."

I heard it once
enter my life,
to rhyme with it in an off-
handed sort of way.
I've been listening ever since.

The gods are up there
and we're down here.
How on earth did they ever
get low enough
to attain that height?

HANDS

The hands of Anderson's
character fluttered
into boys' hair.
Some hands crawl
all the way home

to discover the wrist is gone.
Hands rising into the air
like birds
to be shot down.
The green hand around the heart.

The hand years
in pockets,
its fingers blinded
the day of exit.
The hand meaning

to thrill high
above the crowd,
but forgetting its act.
Hands recurring
in the dreams of snakes.

All the hands
ascended to a
heaven of hands,
all of them applauding
forever.

THE POSITION

A man
down on all fours
with his forehead
touching the earth
is a five.

In that position
he is open
to attack
or love.
Perhaps he is ready

for pushups,
something Western,
athletic, or maybe
he belongs to that tribe
who require their members

always to face
the center of the earth.
It's even possible
he's asleep
and dreaming

of a larger number —
or one
just like him —
into which he can go
and leave nothing over.

9429

NORMANDALE COMMUNITY COLLEGE
9700 FRANCE AVENUE SOUTH
BLOOMINGTON, MN 55431-4399